EARTH AND SPACE SCIENCE

PLATE TECTONICS

By Christina Earley

A Stingray Book

SEAHORSE PUBLISHING

Teaching Tips for Caregivers and Teachers:

This Hi-Lo book features high-interest subject matter that will appeal to all readers in intermediate and middle school grades. It may be enjoyed by students reading at or above grade level as well as by those who are looking for age-appropriate themes matched with a less challenging reading level. Hi-Lo books are ideal for ELL readers, too.

Each book appeals to a striving reader's age and maturity level. Opportunities are provided for students to read words they already know while encountering a limited number of new, high-interest vocabulary words. With these supports in place, students will read more fluently while increasing reading comprehension. Use the following suggestions to help students grow as readers.

- Encourage the student to read independently at home.
- Encourage the student to practice reading aloud.
- Encourage activities that require reading.
- Establish a regular reading time.
- Have the student write questions about what they read.

Teaching Tips for Teachers:

Before Reading

- Ask, "What do I know about this topic?"
- Ask, "What do I want to learn about this topic?"

During Reading

- Ask, "What is the author trying to teach me?"
- Ask, "How is this like something I already know?"

After Reading

- Discuss how the text features (headings, index, etc.) help with understanding the topic.
- Ask, "What interesting or fun fact did you learn?"

TABLE OF CONTENTS

PLATE TECTONICS

The science of plate tectonics describes how Earth's crust is broken up into pieces.

These gigantic sections are called plates. The plates fit together like puzzle pieces. They are always moving at a very slow rate.

Tectonic plates **interact** at their **boundaries** to reshape Earth.

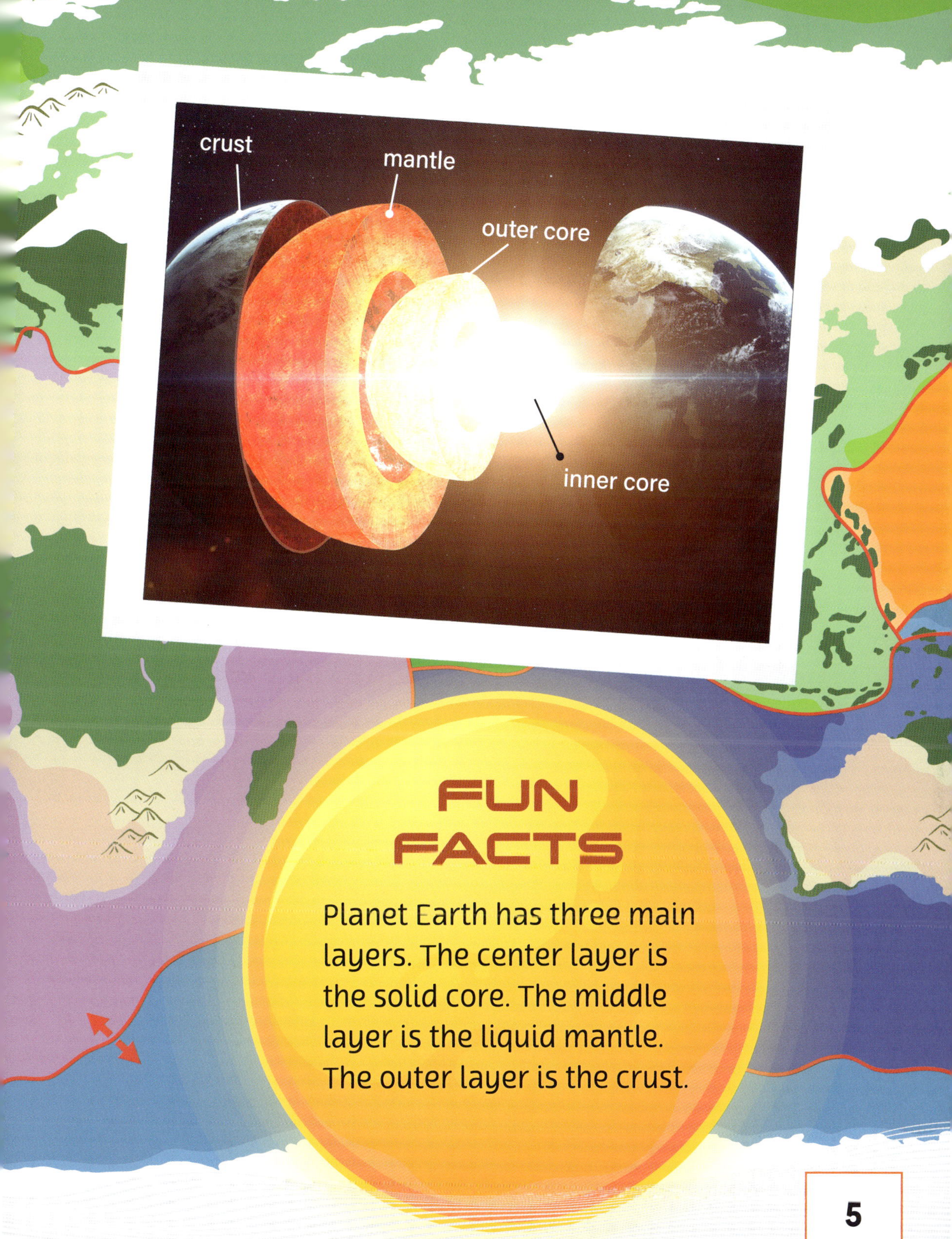

FUN FACTS

Planet Earth has three main layers. The center layer is the solid core. The middle layer is the liquid mantle. The outer layer is the crust.

MAJOR TECTONIC PLATES

Tectonic plates are made of solid rock. They lie under Earth's **continents** and oceans.

The major plates are the African, Antarctic, Eurasian, Indian, Australian, North American, Pacific, and South American plates.

There are also minor tectonic plates and micro tectonic plates.

FUN FACTS

The Pacific Plate is the world's largest. It is 40 million square miles (104 million square kilometers).

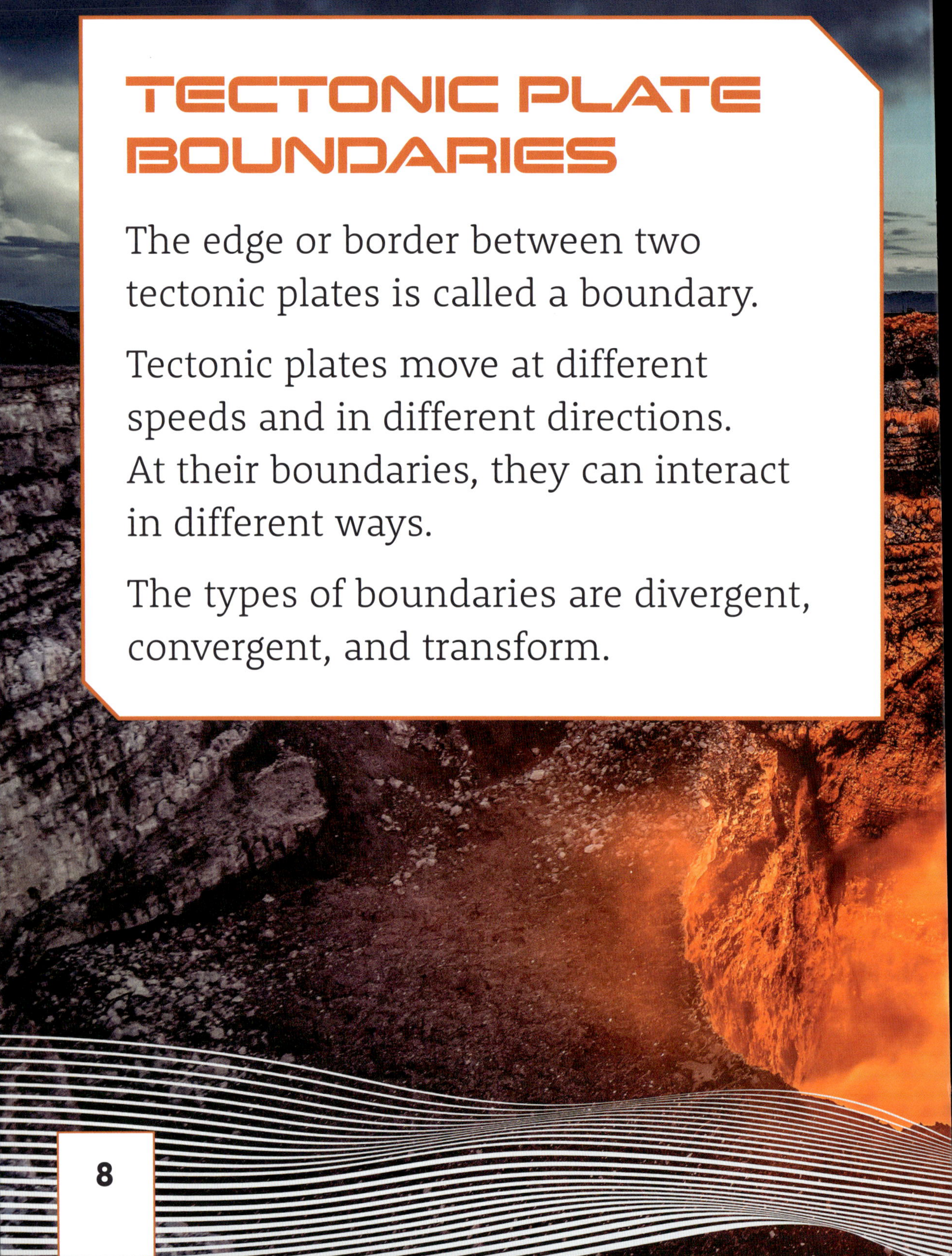

TECTONIC PLATE BOUNDARIES

The edge or border between two tectonic plates is called a boundary.

Tectonic plates move at different speeds and in different directions. At their boundaries, they can interact in different ways.

The types of boundaries are divergent, convergent, and transform.

FUN FACTS

The Ring of Fire is a chain of volcanoes along the boundaries of the Pacific Plate.

DIVERGENT BOUNDARIES

At a divergent boundary, tectonic plates are spreading apart.

This can form **rifts** in the Earth. It can cause earthquakes.

Magma from deep inside Earth rises up to fill the gap between the plates.

New land is formed as the magma cools and hardens.

rift
magma

CONVERGENT BOUNDARIES

At a convergent boundary, tectonic plates are moving toward each other.

As plates **collide**, their edges can get pushed up to form mountains and volcanoes.

When one plate moves under the other, it is called subduction.

Oceanic plates can move under continental plates, forming underwater **trenches**.

FUN FACTS

The Andes Mountain range in South America formed along a convergent boundary.

TRANSFORM BOUNDARIES

At a transform boundary, tectonic plates slide past each other.

The plates grind and scrape together. This can cause faults, or breaks in Earth's crust.

Energy builds up between the plates and gets released in the form of earthquakes.

Unlike divergent and convergent boundaries, transform boundaries do not create new landforms.

FUN FACTS

The San Andreas Fault in California is at a transform boundary between the North American Plate and the Pacific Plate.

CONTINENTAL DRIFT

As tectonic plates move, continents also move. This movement is called continental drift.

Scientists think Earth's continents have joined, broken apart, and moved around throughout the planet's history.

About 270 million years ago, all of Earth's continents were joined in one supercontinent called Pangaea.

CONTINENTAL DRIFT
Pangaea
North America
Europe
Asia
Africa
South America
Australia
Antarctica

CAREER: SEISMOLOGIST

A seismologist studies waves of energy that move through Earth's layers.

These seismic waves come from tectonic movement that causes earthquakes, volcanoes, **tsunamis**, or landslides.

Some seismologists gather information that helps people find oil and other natural resources in Earth's crust.

Computers and **seismographs** help seismologists analyze data.

INVESTIGATE: ORANGE PEEL TECTONIC PLATES

Materials:

- Whole orange with peel
- Plastic knife
- Jam or whipped cream
- Plate (optional)

Procedure:

(1) Carefully peel the orange. Try to remove the peel in one big piece or in a few large pieces. Keep the orange whole. It represents Earth's core.

(2) Spread a layer of jam or whipped cream on the orange. This represents the molten rock, or magma, that makes up Earth's mantle.

(3) Use the knife to cut the peel into three or four pieces. Each piece represents a tectonic plate that makes up Earth's crust.

(4) Carefully put the peels back on the orange.

(5) Slide the peel plates around. Observe what happens at the boundaries between them.

Optional Activity:

(1) Put a scoop of jam or whipped cream on a plate.

(2) Place two smaller orange peels on top.

(3) Push the peels toward each other to create a convergent boundary. Observe.

(4) Push the peels apart to create a divergent boundary. Observe.

(5) Slide the peels past each other to create a transform boundary. Observe.

THE SCIENTIFIC METHOD

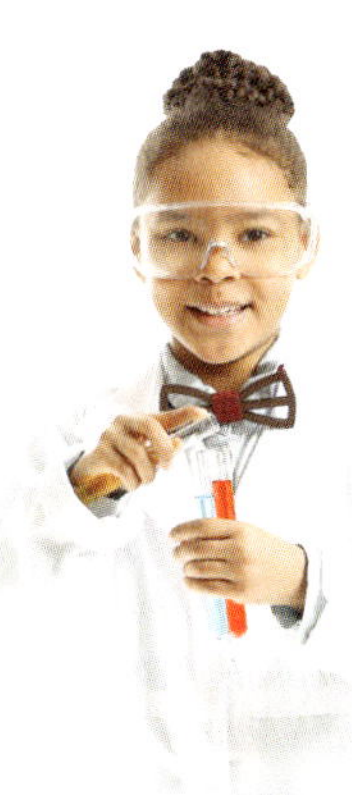

- Ask a question.
- Gather information and observe.
- Make a hypothesis or guess the answer.
- Experiment and test your hypothesis, or guess.
- Analyze your test results.
- Modify your hypothesis, if necessary.
- Make a conclusion.

SCIENTIST SPOTLIGHT

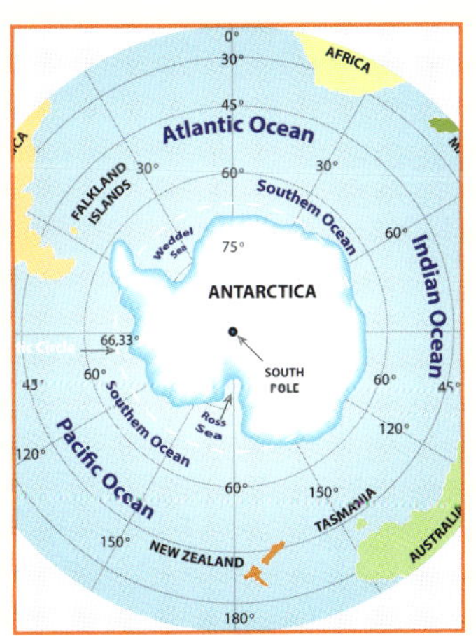

Walter C. Pitman was an American geophysicist. In the 1960s, he demonstrated that the seafloor was spreading. He connected this to the movement of continents. His research proved the theory of plate tectonics. Pitman also wrote some of the first software that allowed ocean researchers to keep data. A seafloor fracture he discovered off Antarctica is named the Pitman Fracture Zone.

GLOSSARY

boundaries (BOUN-dur-eez): edges; places that separate one thing from another

collide (kuh-LIDE): to crash together forcefully

continents (KAHN-tuh-nuhnts): large landmasses on a planet; there are currently seven continents on Earth: Asia, Africa, Europe, North America, South America, Australia, and Antarctica

interact (in-tur-AKT): to react to one another; to become involved with or affect others

magma (MAG-muh): molten and semi-molten rock below Earth's surface that becomes lava when it flows out of volcanoes; magma makes up the layer of Earth called the mantle

oceanic (oh-shee-AN-ik): related to Earth's oceans; oceanic tectonic plates are located beneath oceans

rifts (rifts): cracks or splits in tectonic plates that can form valleys

seismographs (size-MAH-grafs): instruments that detect earthquakes and measure their force

trenches (TRENCH-is): deep ditches

tsunamis (tsu-NAH-mees): huge, destructive waves caused by underwater earthquakes or volcanoes

INDEX

AFTER READING QUESTIONS

1. What are tectonic plates?
2. How do tectonic plates interact to create new landforms?
3. What is continental drift?

ABOUT THE AUTHOR

Christina Earley lives in South Florida with her husband, son, and dog. Her favorite subject in school was science. She enjoys learning the science behind the world around her, such as how roller coasters work. She loves mint chocolate chip ice cream and mermaids.

Written by: Christina Earley
Design by: Kathy Walsh
Editor: Kim Thompson

Library of Congress PCN Data
Plate Tectonics / Christina Earley
Earth and Space Science
ISBN 979-8-8873-5359-3 (hard cover)
ISBN 979-8-8873-5444-6 (paperback)
ISBN 979-8-8873-5529-0 (EPUB)
ISBN 979-8-8873-5614-3 (eBook)
Library of Congress Control Number: 2022951374

Printed in the United States of America.

Photographs/Shutterstock: Cover & Title pg, p 2, 3: fboudrias, Evan Austen, Aksenova Nadezhd, amudsenh; p 5, 7, 9, 13, 15 Hlidskjalf; p 4-23: amudsenh; p 4: BlueRingMedia; p 5: Vadim Sadovski; p 6: Ivan Kuzkin; P 7: Designua; p 8: Roberto Destarac Photo; p 9: Rainer Lesniewskip 10: Photopictures; p 11: stihii; p 12: Guaxinim; p 13: stihii; p 14: Angel McNall Photography; p 15: Luka Veselinovic; p 16: Russ Heinl; p 17: tinkivinki; p 18: IgoZh; p 19: Mila Supinskaya Glashchenko; p 21: deer boy, Pixel-Shot

Seahorse Publishing Company
www.seahorsepub.com

Published in the United States
Seahorse Publishing
PO Box 771325
Coral Springs, FL 33077